ISBN 978-1-333-69876-8
PIBN 10537269

English
Français
Deutsche
Italiano
Español
Português

www.forgottenbooks.com

Mythology Photography **Fiction**
Fishing Christianity **Art** Cooking
Essays Buddhism Freemasonry
Medicine **Biology** Music **Ancient
Egypt** Evolution Carpentry Physics
Dance Geology **Mathematics** Fitness
Shakespeare **Folklore** Yoga Marketing
Confidence Immortality Biographies
Poetry **Psychology** Witchcraft
Electronics Chemistry History **Law**
Accounting **Philosophy** Anthropology
Alchemy Drama Quantum Mechanics
Atheism Sexual Health **Ancient History**
Entrepreneurship Languages Sport
Paleontology Needlework Islam
Metaphysics Investment Archaeology
Parenting Statistics Criminology
Motivational

SUGGESTIONS FOR

EXTERIOR

DECORATION.

H. W. JOHNS M'F'G CO.,

87 MAIDEN LANE, N. Y. *16657⁶*

NEW YORK,
JERSEY CITY,   CHICAGO,
PHILADELPHIA,   BOSTON,
ATLANTA,   LONDON.

8-32130

EXTERIOR DECORATION.

THESE combinations of samples of our Liquid Paints are given as suggestions of proper harmony or contrast and are painted with our Paints as actually supplied to customers. As all colors are affected by sunlight they should be exposed a few hours to the light to perfect the shades.

Of course many other desirable combinations may be made with the various shades and tints shown on our Sample Sheets. Those desiring special or more elaborate combinations may obtain them free, from any of our offices, or from dealers in our Paints, upon indicating the colors they wish to use. When desired, we shall be pleased to give our customers the benefit of our experience in selecting for their dwellings appropriate combinations of colors.

H. W. JOHNS M'F'G CO.

SUGGESTIONS IN REGARD TO DESIRABLE SHADES AND TRIMMINGS.

For dwellings in elevated or exposed situations, our dark grays, drabs, olives and other dark colors are most desirable. For dwellings not so situated, or which are surrounded by shade trees, the yellows, reds, and light tints are preferable.

When the ornamental work (mouldings, cornices, etc.) is heavy, i. e., presents a large surface. the lighter trimming shades should be used, but when light and graceful in design, the darker trimming shades are more effective. For window sashes, Dark, Bright or Pompeian Reds, Maroon, Bronze or Olive Green, Olive, etc., are generally used ; and Browns or Dark Reds may be used with good effect where warm yellows are used on buildings.

The following combinations of our liquid Paints are selected with a view to harmony. In making selection, due consideration must be given to style of architecture, surroundings, etc.

BODY COLORS.	TRIMMINGS.	BLINDS.
89, 90, 91, 92 or 44,	Outside White or 35,	Outside White or 62.
20,	43,	62,
22,	25, / Outside White,	53, / 25, 62 or Outside White.
30,	52 or 59,	51.
76,	45, 35 or 33,	53. 51 or 62
77,	43,	64, 60, 73. 68,
81,	27 or 46,	53, 52, 66,
82,	92, 89, 44,	60, 65, 53, 62,
43,	64 or 68,	73, 60, 62,
45,	54 or 66,	51 or 60,
33.	35, 27 26,	53, 51,
46,	26 or 54.	65, 51, 53,
42, 31 or 87,	28, 29, 53,	51, 62,
19,	45, 46, 26.	53. 73. 68, 51,
27,	26, 66. 54,	53, 51, 65,
35,	82, / 45,	65, / 53,
58,	53,	73,
59,	53.	51,

The yellows which are so extensively used on Colonial and other styles of houses, should be trimmed with our Outside White. For Blinds and Sash, use No. 62, Dark Green or Outside white. In order to meet the demand for a more subdued combination than the ordinary Colonial Yellows and White, we are now supplying our customers with Ivory White, which, for trimmings and blinds, in combination with Nos. 19, 33, 89, 20, 22, 76, 81, 92, 44, 35 or 25, produces a very soft and harmonious effect. With these combinations Ivory White or No. 62, Dk. Green may be used for sash and blinds.

Body colors of light greys and other neutral tints may also be trimmed with White or Ivory White, using same color for blinds and sash.

When two colors are used on large, plain surfaces, a dividing line of some contrasting color should be drawn between them, unless the first story body color is of some strong, rich shade, as No. 60, 53, etc. Usually in such cases, the first story body color is used for trimmings on second story, no trimming color being necessary on first story.

Our STANDARD GREEN may be advantageously used for blinds with White or the following body colors : No. 44, 45, 33, 19 and 35.

A perfect representation of brown stone and Nova Scotia stone may be produced by sanding Nos. 34 and 19 respectively.

The prevailing taste for certain styles of architecture demands the use of shingles, either wholly or in part, and for this work we recommend the use of our Shingle Stains. These are made from the purest pigments and the best wood preservative known. While the treatment of shingle staining is more simple than painted work, fewer and less vivid colors being used, there is great necessity of experienced judgment, as in addition to harmony of color, the element of effect is largely to be considered. Almost all work of this kind should be specially treated, and to those wishing suggestions we shall be glad to lend every assistance upon receipt of photograph or full description of buildings and surroundings. We have aimed to produce with our Shingle stains, many desirable tones of silver gray, moss green, and other weather stained effects.

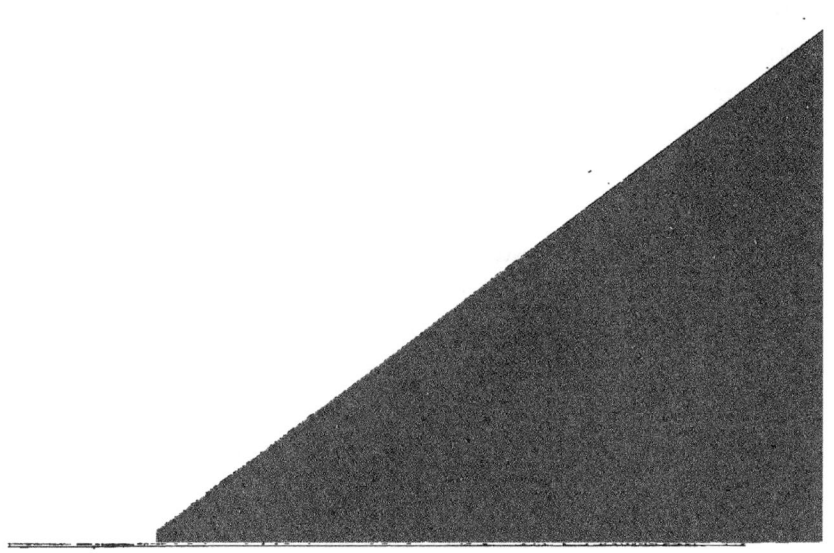

ASBESTOS·

H. W. JOHNS' LIQUID PAINTS.

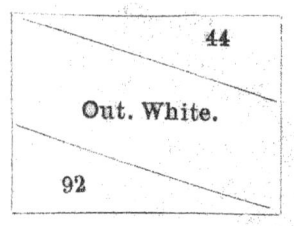

No. 92, Light Colonial,

or

No. 44, Cream.

TRIMMINGS FOR THESE SHADES SHOULD BE OF OUR OUTSIDE WHITE. BLINDS AND SASH, No. 62, DARK GREEN, OR OUTSIDE WHITE.

ASBESTOS

H. W. JOHNS' LIQUID PAINTS.

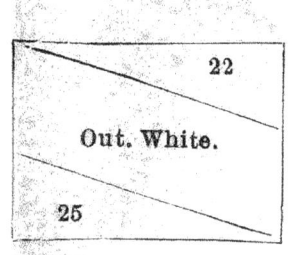

Body Color, Shade No. 25, Ex. Lt. Drab, or No. 22, Pearl Gray.

Trimmings,   - -   Outside White.

Blinds, &c.,   -   "   "

Sash,   -   -   "   "

or No. 62, Dk. Green.

DESIGN PATENTED.

ASBESTOS·

H. W. JOHNS' LIQUID PAINTS.

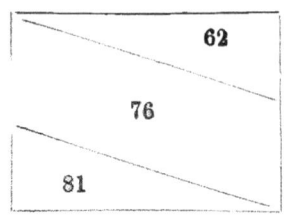

Body Color, Shade No. 76, PINK DRAB.

Trimmings,   "   "   81, LT. YELLOW DRAB

Blinds, &c.,   "   "   62, DARK GREEN.

Sash,   "   "   62, DARK GREEN.

ASBESTOS

H. W. JOHNS' LIQUID PAINTS.

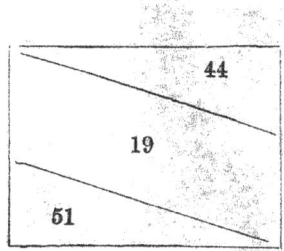

Body Color, Shade No. 19, Light Stone.

Trimmings,   "   "   44, Cream.

Blinds, &c.,   "   "   51, Maroon.

Sash,   "   "   51, Maroon.

DESIGN PATENTED.

H. W. JOHNS' LIQUID PAINTS.

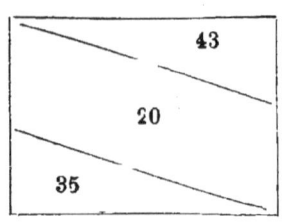

Body Color, Shade No. 20, GREEN STONE.

Trimmings,   "   "   35, BUFF.

Blinds, &c.,   "   "   43, LT. OLIVE DRAB.

Sash,   "   "   62, DARK GREEN.

8

H . W . JOHNS' LIQUID PAINTS.

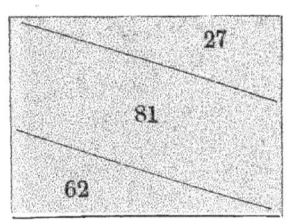

Body Color, Shade No. 81, Lt. Yellow Drab.

Trimmings,   "   "   27, Med. Drab.

Blinds, &c.,   "   "   62, Dark Green.

Sash,   "   "   62, Dark Green.

DESIGN PATENTED.

ASBESTOS

H. W. JOHNS' LIQUID PAINTS.

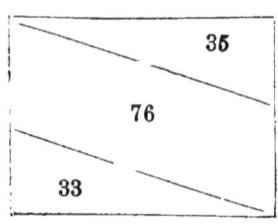

Body Color, Shade No. 76, PINK DRAB.

Trimmings,   "   " 35, BUFF.

Blinds, &c.,   "   " 33, YELLOW DRAB.

Sash,   ."   " 18, BLACK.

H. W. JOHNS' LIQUID PAINTS.

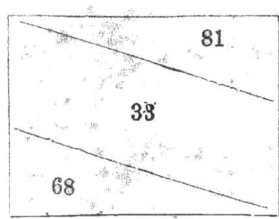

Body Color, Shade No. 33, YELLOW DRAB.

Trimmings,   "   "   81, LT. YELLOW DRAB.

Blinds, &c.   "   "   68, LT. OLIVE GREEN.

Sash,   "   "   73, POMPEIAN RED.

DESIGN PATENTED.

AS the cost of applying paint will average twice the cost of the material, it is of great importance that the paint employed should be of the best possible quality, as the trifling additional outlay for material will be many times repaid by the superior durability and satisfactory appearance of a first-class article.

Ours are the only prepared or liquid paints which, in addition to the usual grinding and mixing, are ground while in liquid state.

This second grinding brings the oil and pigments into more intimate combination, and gives a uniformity of consistence not to be obtained by mere mixings.

Strictly first-class paints are more economical to the user and more desirable for the dealer, and we shall continue to spare no pains or expense to insure for our Paints the reputation they have long held, as

"THE STANDARD PAINTS FOR STRUCTURAL PURPOSES."

We will be pleased to forward by mail, on application, samples of 56 newest shades and colors, with instructions for using, price list, etc.

Liquid Priming,
       Shingle Stains,
          Liquid Dryer,
Liquid Coach Colors,   **Fine Colors in Oil,**
       Wood Stains,
          Asbestos Roof Cement,
4-19-93.   **Iron=Oxide Paint.**

CPSIA information can be obtained
at www.ICGtesting.com
Printed in the USA
LVHW081926100119
603305LV00043B/760/P

9 781333 698768